PROFIT | PROPHET

—

Patrick Blagrave

Profit | Prophet by Patrick Blagrave
ISBN: 9798550419137

Written by Patrick Blagrave.
Editing and cover design by Terra Oliveira.

Cover image: A newspaper photograph of an internal staircase in the
Asch Building after the Triangle Shirtwaist Factory fire. New York, 1911.

Image source: The Kheel Center Collection: International Ladies
Garment Workers Union Photographs (1885-1985)

Published in December 2020 by Recenter Press.

www.patrickblagrave.com
www.recenterpress.com

To a future
without profit.

CONTENTS

—

PROFIT

"What profit is there in my blood?" — *Psalm 30:9*

I've done the math as well as I can.
Every month I work an estimated
140 hours. The landlord
does not work but instead 38 hours
I work are for him. Worse, 65 hours
are accounted for by student loans &
10 hours by credit card payments. The company
that pays me uses me as a vessel
to move money to other companies.
My wallet stays empty. For 4 days each month
my work is done for me to have money
to eat, drink, buy a sweater or to waste
in a bank. My boss takes another trip,
thinks I can live like this, that we both can.

Coworkers talk 401(k)s. Some people
are so eager to explain compound interest.
My family warns me about emergency
savings. A well-meaning friend with a mortgage
tells me I should buy a house too because
rent will keep going up & pretty soon
I won't be able to afford to live
here. Often I couldn't. The past keeps you
from affording the future. The balance:
        $160,000 —— Navient
        $68,000 —— Great Lakes (forbearance)
        $6300 —— Capital One
        $4700 —— Citibank
        $3200 —— credit union

When confronting an unpayable debt
generated by war Richard Nixon
in 1971 did not end
the war but the direct relationship
of the dollar to gold & ever since
money hasn't had any intrinsic value.

On the radio this morning a voice
without a body said the kilogram
the last unit of measurement tied to
a tangible object would be defined
no longer by a perfect piece of platinum
in a vault where it imperceptibly
degraded but by math I can't understand.

Our history is one of hollowing.

They profit off my need to have a home.
They profit while I sleep. When I wake up
everything I do is for their profit.
They profit off my decision not to
freeze in winter. They profit off my thirst
& my hunger & the cheap clothes I wear.
They profit off every dollar in the bank
& every time my account is empty.
They profit when I get sick but they profit
anyway when I'm healthy. If I die
before we make them change they will profit
finally off grief. More than anything
they profit off misery; if you're happy
you're probably one of them, profiting.

In the room where we remove still-tied shoes,
where we have warm oatmeal & hot coffee,
where I recovered from injuries with
a cat laying on top of where it hurt

& in the room where in the morning I
feed the cats & make oatmeal & coffee
& where I taught myself to fill a place
with the smell of freshly baked bread or smoke

& in the room where I sleep & you sleep
or don't sleep & where we struggle to wake
& where our tooth-brushed mouths find each other
& where above the bed we hung a print

of a small white house alone near water
we imagine we're living in our home.

In the countryside, million dollar homes.
In the city, the same. The same people
own all of them. A check for a thousand
dollars sits on a polished wood table
in a spotless entryway for two weeks.

Our landlords might have complicated lives,
beautiful, heartbreaking relationships
like the ones in award-winning novels
we've been told people weep over, the kind
we were taught to believe are important.

They want us to think this but we shouldn't.
Every piece of art is propaganda
& the kind we're told is good is useful
to the wrong people. They have our money.

They say that you can't escape your past but
what they mean is that you can't afford to.

The past grows larger every new day:
        unpaid interest on the original
        sin of being born to the wrong bank account.
Instead of a future I have a debt,
        a career, morning alarms, monthly
        calls with collectors to look forward to.
Not a future but an overdue rent
check, a reckoning, a careful schedule
of humiliations. Not a future, but
a promise that demands not to be kept.

What they mean is you can never escape
the futurelessness assigned to you.

In 2008 I was in a class
on 19th century literature
reading some novels about rich people
desperately trying to keep their money
when one day the economy collapsed!
Companies we let so much depend on
were suddenly closing. Bankers panicked
& convinced everyone else to panic.

We're asked in so many ways to believe
that no longer being rich is the worst
thing that could ever happen to someone.
It's a well-written story, perfected
over centuries. They always get what
they want. This is not a happy ending.

My classes were taught in what was once
the Triangle Shirtwaist Factory where
in a fire 100 years earlier
146 people were killed—
mostly women: immigrants, teenagers.
The owners kept the doors locked to prevent
unscheduled breaks. The foreman with keys saved
himself before thinking to unlock them.
The owners were put on trial & escaped
consequences. They opened more factories.
They profited off the insurance claims.
They kept locking doors. In these same rooms
I was trained how to be above all else
a good worker, how to ignore the ghosts.

Inside the offices of Capital
where I work at the end of the world
I prepare documentation proving
that everything can be saved. Don't worry
about the people that you stepped over;
don't worry about the waves; don't worry
you can't afford to go to the doctor
who you think wants to kill you anyway.

A company pays him to kill slowly.
A company pays me to live slightly
longer into the future they have planned.

The future looks like the new work schedule
& it is bright & early. Every morning
we make money to pay for the afternoon.

There is a future without me in it.
I spend my whole life searching for this one
moment when light will shine from the pencil
marks on my page just right. It will be
raining or it won't be. Lights reflecting
off whatever is in the way. I am
in the way of the most useful ending:
a future that is empty of the work
I do to pay the rent; empty of rent,
corporations & the endless amount
I owe them erased from all books, these words
indecipherable & these pages
not yet dust & me not yet dust, not yet
worthless. This is something else that I owe.

Whether the future is a struggle to
rise out of oppression or just from bed
today I rise with trouble & I walk
into the offices of Capital
to work in Sinner City & it takes
years each day, my body beating against
concrete then keyboards, my body sold off
to Capital. They pay me in installments
to move as directed. Since I don't own it
I sabotage Capital's possession:
I drink too much, eat badly, don't sleep. Each day,

with sincere thanks to unions, I dedicate
8 hours to hating work, 8 to dreading
work, 8 to what I will come to regret.

They'd have you believe happiness is nice
in theory but never works if you just
look at the history. Economists
assure us we can't afford it at least
not in my lifetime & I should live for
a long time but that isn't up to me.

I sell myself piecemeal by the hour.
I sell misery at market value
& every hour become more useless.
I make nothing except some money &
none of it lasts & America will
never know how much to take. The current
system is one of rarified relief:
I drop cream into coffee; it's my break.

If I had to buy shoes for work I lost
a week of groceries. I heated beans
in a roommate's skillet or went to bed
instead, woke up early, got warm pretzels
3 for a dollar on Washington Ave
walking to work in dry socks to last all day.

I remember the day I let myself
own more than 1 pair of shoes, 2 jackets
for different cool weather outfits. It felt
comfortable, just like any betrayal.

While I'm confessing let me also say
without the accent I had growing up
that I've hoarded enough now to stay warm
& it feels very good & it feels bad.

I've done the math as well as I can.   1
I won't be able to afford to live   2
When confronting an unpayable debt   3
& every time my account is empty.   4

feed the cats & make oatmeal & coffee   5
beautiful, heartbreaking relationships   6

Instead of a future I have a debt,   7
We're asked in so many ways to believe   8
consequences. They opened more factories.   9
where I work at the end of the world   10
in the way of the most useful ending: 11
today I rise with trouble & I walk   12
& every hour become more useless.   13
& it feels very good & it feels bad.   14

They've been circulating long enough   17
employees deserving extra money   18
to know: who not to trust & to worry   19
for the last time. To keep believing in   20
naturally, your home, your friends & loved ones.   21
It happened before. Whether we see it   22
if things fall apart; we know better.   23
could be anything, bright as sun & flames.   24
looking down from the observation deck.   25
taller than the houses & the churches.   26
in a locked glass temperature-controlled room.   27
but its windows are replaced by still air.   28
be replaced. When retaking what's been lost   29
& they'll miss me & they'll talk about me—   30

There is a mouth on every coin, every dollar.
Alexander Hamilton—hold him close enough
& he'll whisper that he's in love with banks.

The larger denominations are more
persuasive; whoever holds them can hear
constant voices in their heads: *swallow   bite
kill*.   The work of mouths: take from other mouths.

They've been circulating long enough
the commands, now static in the background
of each American interaction.

Put a penny to your tongue, you'll taste blood
but try it with a hundred dollar bill,
taste the blood of everyone who suffered
so you could get it; hear them cheer for you.

Sometime soon Jeff Bezos could become history's
first trillionaire. On the platform of a
different billionaire I spend my evening
arguing with strangers about Whole Foods
employees deserving extra money
& protection while keeping stores open
during a pandemic. They're demanding
double pay. Amazon's making record
profits while so many die. This person
thinks they should be happy with what they get.
Ridiculous, he says, to get double.
Jeff Bezos has never been happy with
what he takes. We should all demand so much
more, not demand that others demand less.

Things come so easily to some people,
it almost seems like it's an accident.

Worrying, I tell a loved one not to
worry; subtly, they betray that they don't

know there is something to worry about.
This slip up is the only accident:

shaky solipsism of secret comfort.
There is no excuse not to be self-made

& I am, into living resentment,
meaning my family gave me all I needed

to know: who not to trust & to worry
whenever my bank account or belly

are full it wasn't meant to happen &
people are working to correct the error.

Already by 1979
the future was over everywhere but
on Wall St where boring men can still buy
& sell things they call futures hoping for
a crash they're free from the consequences of.
Like oil or like water, everything
from the past gets transmuted in this
economy into harm in the air.
We are breathing in endless profit.
When it rains ticker tape it is always
for the last time. To keep believing in
any kind of ending, even one like
tomorrow gets harder every day.
It comes, & we deal with it well enough.

A modern Job, a balancing act by
higher powers constantly pushing you
ever closer to despair, to the point
just before you lose faith in the system
they devised. If you lose, lose everything:
health insurance if you had it then health
naturally, your home, your friends & loved ones.
You can sit in the ash when it settles
& curse the gods who sit behind closed doors
& decide your future for you. Wail proof
that you exist but they already know—
you're not forsaken, they found a new use.
Detail your disaster on their forms. Ask
for their pity, as if pity's enough.

Neruda said *you can cut all the flowers*
but you cannot keep spring from coming
but the season gets shorter every year.
Sometimes the daffodils will die before
anybody has the chance to see them.
Their genes have been patented by DuPont.
Governments have sold the rights to weather
to some oil & gas executives.
They are scheming at HAARP to make it so
the earth will become an endless golf course.
The sun goes on aging invisibly.
The earth will become an endless ocean.
It happened before. Whether we see it
or not the next spring will be beautiful.

In the 80s they said it would come down
in a trickle. In the 90s they said
there isn't a need for a safety net.
After 9/11 they asked people
for their support extracting resources
& killing millions in the Middle East,
& to go into debt & buy houses,
& when the terms were revealed to be bad
they said you should have known better than that.
In 2008 as they have all along
they said that they needed all of the help
to go to those at the top, otherwise
things would fall apart. It doesn't matter
if their things fall apart; we know better.

Across the street from Philly's city hall
every day masses of people walked past
a statue of Frank Rizzo, former police
commissioner & mayor, bigot & brute.

Inside mayor Jim Kenney proposed
increased funding to the police dept.
at the cost of public health, libraries,
homeless services, streets, parks & the arts.

Masses of people protested for days
& more, & the statue looked on,
spray painted & pried at, as cop cars were
set on fire on Broad in broad daylight
& as long as they burned the future
could be anything, bright as sun & flames.

I saw the skyline turn to glare: gold &
pink then entirely away from me.

The buildings are named things like Liberty
& Liberty & Comcast & Comcast.

They are built for businesses & condos
& windows that show us even the clouds
in this part of town belong to others.

Liberty is luxury offices
& a lookout point tourists can pay for.

From the street on a perfectly clear day
& from almost every neighborhood
in the city you can see exactly
how invisible anyone must be
looking down from the observation deck.

A neon sign for check cashing & loans.
A neon sign for cold Miller High Life.
A chain link fence around an unkept park.
Father teaching son how to hold a bat.
A gap in the fence, cracks in the sidewalk.
A neon sign for no credit at all.
Dead neon letters on the grocery store.
A stapled paper sign for a lost dog.
A woodpecked telephone pole. A valley
of grass & cages, gnarled metal structures
taller than the houses & the churches.
A weathered For Sale sign on a front lawn
& a small pile of dirt beside it
from someone having just buried a saint.

The dry cleaner's replaced by a cafe.
The shoe repair's replaced by a cafe.
The bakery's replaced by a brewery.
The barber's replaced by a restaurant.
The hardware store's replaced by a wine bar.
The florist's replaced by a bottle shop.
The bodega's replaced by ATMs
in a locked glass temperature-controlled room.
The factory's replaced by a warehouse
is replaced by an arts space is replaced
by a row of luxury apartments.
The houses are replaced by apartments.
Black neighbors are replaced by white neighbors.
All neighbors left replaced by investors.

The laundromat's replaced by check cashing.
The grocery store's replaced by a bank.
The gas station's shut down & boarded up.
The diner's replaced by a fast food chain.
The thrift store's replaced by a dollar store.
The public schools reopen as charter schools.
The hospital's closed & isn't replaced
& the doctors relocated downtown.
The factory's closed & isn't replaced
but its windows are replaced by still air.
A facade is replaced by scaffolding.
A house is replaced by a fallen house.
Those who can leave are replaced by those who can't.
The neighbors are replaced by their own ghosts.

A Target is not a community.
A Target stands on top of what was once
a community. A police precinct
is not a part of a community
or its safety. A neighbor can be your
community but maybe not if they
live in new construction or are a cop.
A Dunkin' or McDonald's can be where
better cheap options have already been
replaced by a Dunkin' or McDonald's.
It happens all the time & there's no where
else to go. Any of these buildings can
be replaced. When retaking what's been lost
do not be peaceful but please take care.

I will have been a productive worker
& an asset to my employer
& other workers will have liked me too
& they'll miss me & they'll talk about me—
how well I worked & how congenial.

I will have lived for most of my life
uneasily though sometimes almost well.
She'll have been there with me & that's enough.

I will have spent countless hours working
& spent a carefully counted amount
of money, enriched plenty of others,
served—as well as I could—America.

I do not expect to be forgiven.
I will have never wanted to forgive.

PROPHET

*"Somebody else's idea of things to come
need not be the only way
to vision the future"* — *Sun Ra*

*"Metaphorically speaking, the people
are like water"* — *Mao Zedong*

I. VESSELS

a voice
a wilderness
wild honey-
scented

—/—

a voice
made trembling
water into something better
than home

the Delaware River
no matter how close you are
never roars

even when I am
roaring

like I need to
scare a god
back into
cracked porcelain
hands

—/—

a voice
a god
spilling out
into the water

water spilling out
of failing hands

the broken cups of my hands
such poor vessels

—/—

a hand reaches down
into the river
& breaks
the waves
& even that
is some small ending

—/—

hands find meaning
only in work
are vessels for work
are not built
to hold on for long

—/—

*where do you imagine
yourself in 5 years?*
        in 10 years?

work so often insists
we believe that
nothing will end
or more importantly

nothing else will begin

—/—

up at the alarm
to give up
more every morning
of my belongings
to those owed

I dreamt of leaving
to go where the wild
honey is abundant
& affordable

—/—

it happened before

—/—

up at the alarm
to give up
dreaming

when in a dream so often
it is taken as a warning
never remembered

the day is already
laid out for me
on the bed
& I wear it

as if it were a good deal
better than other options
& curse the reflection

—/—

once I woke up
& walked into the water

I left my phone,
my wallet, my shoes
        on a ledge

my heaviest books
in my largest pockets

I let the river take over
what I could not manage: living
without knowing how
it would end

—/—

what is a prophet
but a person
who doesn't accept
what looks like
the future

—/—

all the possibilities
I pretended I had

& I just wanted to know
how it would end

I taught myself
all the endings

—/—

now the lights flicker
in the only house
left open to me

—/—

now a sudden crack
in the arctic

—/—

now it's the first
week of the month
& it's snowing
& the rent costs
$370 plus the heat
which who knows
in January
in what is likely to be
the warmest year
again

—/—

now it's 30 years
later & I can't remember
snow or the cinnamon rolls
I made with my wife
that morning or the cat
becoming less
of a kitten

—/—

now I am headless
a body
stretched across
what was once
a river

a river
that was once
my god

—/—

what is a prophet
but a person
who sees their god
evaporating

—/—

what is a god
but our best plans
a list of the dreams of the past

such poor vessels

—/—

now I am mindless

home from an office
after writing reports
that keep me alive
& I have no wants left

I wanted to write prophecies

these are just reports

—/—

II. RESOURCE

the prophet John
a head held
in his hands
enacts an ending
      (the waves break over you)
allows a beginning
      (the sky through a filter)
allows another ending
      (the waves unfold around you)

—/—

a convincing
practice
a ritual
submersion
one's very own flood myth

a small helpful glimpse
into an apocalypse

it is good to seek out endings

to know you're allowed to
keep living

—/—

the most pure thing
you can do in life
is to start a new one
devoted to

shouting at the king

leave your homes
& the thoughts you belong to
& when the king comes around
laugh through mouths
stuck on honey
until you feel mercy

—/—

the prophet John
a head held
up to the walls
of the palace
cistern

listening for the beating
of the wings
of the angel of death

listening for the footsteps
of his followers
wanting to save him
the clatter of their arms

the cistern
collects the rain
so all he hears is rain
& all he feels is godless
rain the wrong kind of water
trickle down

no longer the vessel
through which purifying
voices within him
pass to water

but silent within one
reserved with damp
echoes & other wild
waters to soothe
the throat of a king

only knowing the future
is rare & his bleak
soon to be traded around
by his rulers
same as anyone else

it's a debt
the future always is
overwhelming

& he knows this
& he pleads
please
take my head
in your hands
so I don't
drown in it

—/—

her hand
on his cheek
          his body
          out of reach

if alive he would
smell flowers
          a bloom smears
          from its stem

if allowed he would

see how beautiful
      the body is
      spreading

red over
palace walls

—/—

the prophet John
a head held
aloft
on a platter
having never touched
in his life
silver

how cold

—/—

III. PROPHECIES

I stood near the river
& the sky blackened over Philadelphia

& I saw above me
a powerful fire

in wide columns spread
over the river & fiery

letters could be read in it
as if it were to brand the skin of the water

in neon the letters spelled
AMERICAN WATER

& I saw from on the land
illuminated by the fire

a body in the water
standing waist high in it

dark waves of hair reaching the water
& spreading out wide where they met

bright red lips could be seen
& their eyes were black pools

& the person turned to me
& shouted & when they spoke

water cascaded from their opening
red lips & blood from their neck

cascaded & mixed with the water
& fell into the river

& they said to me
"you fucking assholes

don't you realize what's been going on here?
don't you care at all? jesus christ"

confused & affronted by the outburst
I turned to leave though it was a startling sight

& was stopped as they continued
to shout to me & all nearby

"don't you hear that
the sound of the wings?"

& as they said this I began to hear
ferocious whirling as from many helicopters

& at the same time felt a strong wind
pushing against me from across the river

"don't you smell that
the scent of the burning?"

& as they said this a thick smoke could be seen
in the wind & clogged my breathing

"don't you know what's above you—
how terrible?"

& they pulled a hand from out of the river
& pointed urgently to the sky above

the burning & there I saw
where there had been a void of night

a great monstrous being
& it was in the form of

BlackRock Investment Management Company
CEO Larry Fink

unmistakable & large
as any building in the city

& held over it by the ceaseless wheels
of rotating blades that were his wings

& in his right hand he gripped a great war
machine & the fingers

of his left hand were countless parallel
metal bars like from many prison cells

& when he spoke
it was 100 times louder

than if the voice of every other person
upon the earth were to sound at once

& he shrieked "I keep mankind alive"
& repeated the phrase endlessly

it was terrible
the person in the river

seemed to continue to shout & gesture
& blood & water continued to flow

heavily from their neck & mouth
though I could no longer hear their words

over the noise of the wings & proclamation
of the hideous being that now controlled

all the dark horizon & all attention
& this went on for some time

—/—

eventually the one who warned us appeared
to lose strength & to struggle to remain upright in the water

upon seeing this finally I knew
what was to be done

for the first time since the chaos began
& I leapt into the river

& was submerged beneath the violent
waves but it was cool

& it washed me clean of the soot
& it washed my senses clean

of the burning smell & burning wind
& it muted the thundering voice

& I felt a sense of clarity
disturbed only by the realization of others

plunging into the river as well
all of us swimming to save

the one who first made us aware
of the danger hovering above us

who was saved by myself & several strangers
working together & pulled to the shore

—/—

now by this time police had arrived
& demanded we remove ourselves

from the property of American Water Works
an important asset of BlackRock

& continue to stand in awe
of the terrible creature before us

but they were ignored by all
who found protection in the water

& at intervals the demonic presence of Larry Fink
would attack from his hand that was a weapon

or gather innocents in his hand that was a prison
targeting all below him

& people were dying or being taken
though they soon began to seek shelter together

& to hold on to each other in long chains
though they were strangers previously

& this did keep some tethered to safety
& the power & reach of the creature was great

—/—

when resuscitated the person
whose long dark hair covered their body

whose eyes were black pools
& whose lips were brightest red

pulled me down so my face met theirs
& said to me

"all it takes to know the future
is to know the future doesn't change

unless you work to change it
so what the fuck are you waiting for

you saved me & you're saving each other
you can save everyone"

& with that the pools of their eyes emptied
& their mouth turned pale

& the last amounts of blood
trickled down from around their neck

—/—

such was my encounter
& I & many of the strangers around me

were moved to warn others
about the dangers above us

& to work to keep each other safe
& to devote ourselves

to changing the circumstances
that allowed such terrors to exist

because of our experience
& what was revealed to us:

that we could end our worlds
& live in different ones

that we hold them all
in our failing hands

—/—

ACKNOWLEDGEMENTS

—

Thank you to Terra Oliveira for believing in this book & for all the work they did to make it better & real.

Thank you to the editors of *Recenter Press Poetry Journal*, *Peace, Land, and Bread*, *Bedfellows*, & *Mad House* for publishing versions of these poems.

Thank you to Alina Pleskova, Angelo Colavita, John Wall Barger, Kevin Travers, & Royce Drake for their expert advice, & to the many friends & peers from Poetry Nights who inspired, supported, & shaped my writing over the years.

Thank you to Emma for always reading & reassuring me about my work & our futures.

ABOUT THE AUTHOR

—

Patrick Blagrave is a poet, editor, and debtor from
Philadelphia. His work often explores capitalism's
cruelty and absurdity, and tries to imagine better
futures without it. Some of his writing has been
published in *Peace, Land, and Bread*, *SORTES*,
Recenter Press Poetry Journal, *Mad House Maga-
zine*, *Apiary*, and *Bedfellows*.

Prolit Magazine, the literary journal he founded in
2019, publishes writing and art explicitly centered
around money, work, and class. It can be found at
www.prolitmag.com.

Recenter Press is a Philadelphia-based publisher
dedicated to sharing work that documents personal
transformation, that speaks to the need for the
revolutionary transformation of society, and
captures our deep communion with the world.

Thank you for sharing this space with us.

—

re-centering:

*to cut through deception and
heal our alienation; to bring ourselves closer
to Love, to Truth, and to Liberation.*

—

More from Recenter Press:
Doe Parker - *The Good House & The Bad House*
Terra Oliveira - *And Still To Sleep* and *An Old Blue Light*
Schuyler Peck - *To Hold Your Moss-Covered Heart*

Manufactured by Amazon.ca
Bolton, ON